HIGH WATER

Poems by
Carrie Carter

QUILLKEEPERS PRESS

Copyright © Carrie Carter, 2023
Cover Design by David Wojciechowski
Edit by Stephanie Lamb
Format by Quillkeepers Press, LLC

All rights reserved. No part of this book may be reproduced in any form or by any electronic or mechanical means, including information storage and retrieval systems, without the permission in writing from the publisher, except by a reviewer who may quote brief passages in a review.

This compilation contains some works of fiction. Locales and public names are sometimes used for atmospheric purposes. Any resemblance to actual people, living or dead, or to businesses, companies, events, institutions, or locales are completely coincidental. Any references to pop culture are owned by their specific companies and are not the property of the author.

There are some poems here within that represent thoughts of the author. Any resemblance to actual events, locals, or persons, living or dead, is entirely coincidental.

ISBN: 979-8-9868389-7-7

Published by Quillkeepers Press, LLC
PO Box 10236
Casa Grande, AZ 85130

For James,
who gives me both time, and space.

CONTENTS

I love you. I love you,
but I'm turning to my verses
and my heart is closing
like a fist.

-     *Frank O'Hara*

Ecopoetic

I failed the birds this year.
Every day the cardinal comes to my kitchen
window to ask for food. I have none.
My friends call to ask if I am eating.

My former colleagues can read the carbon cycle.
The ones with children say there is nothing to worry
about. On the timeline, another hate crime, another
law reversed. My friends call to ask if I am eating.

Fruit set on my tomato vines are like a core sample.
It rains too hard for the downspouts.
Glaciers melt, rivers dry
but the fin whales return to the south pole
and I don't eat, and I don't cry.

Grandmother's Teapot

One time I got my hand stuck
in my grandmother's teapot.
For a moment, there was fear
that I would have to break   the teapot.
I wondered what it meant
to break your grandmother's   teapot.
Who would offer wabi-sabi
and who would say bad juju?
For a moment I thought about
just leaving it. Red ceramic fist
that I got from my grandmother.
It is the only object I have of her
from her home, where I spent so much
time with her, helping her husband die.

No one touched him in the hospital.
They just stood near him, a monolith of grief.
My father took my grandmother to lunch
one afternoon, so I scooted the chair
to the side of my grandfather's bed
got myself a blanket from the hallway cart
sat, reached over, and held his frigid hand
attached to his shell.
He is just a dying human, nothing more frightening
than that. He deserves love too.

The red ceramic fist that I got from my grandmother
finally slides off my hand. The next day there is
a small ring of bruise at the base. I will make tea
that day, and every day, as long as I have the
teapot.

2

Decades

Living with the people who come in and out of your life.
Living with the young ones and the dead ones.
Living with your own wisdom.

Teaching the young ones to set clear intentions.
Teaching the young ones gratitude.
Teaching the young ones.

Remembering the dead ones who taught you clarity.
Remembering the dead ones who taught you hope.
Remembering the dead ones.

How do you manifest when you are still healing?
How do you offer risk, knowing what you could lose?
How do you teach yourself to live by remembering?

Desire

I wanted you to do to me
what the snow does
to a landscape.

Time

Finally, after weeks of rain,
the windows open and the crickets sing.
All summer I have been fighting everything with a steel heart:
doors that won't close,
my mother's head a timpani down the stairs,
the smoke detector in the kitchen,
the city,
the landlord,
my father's pain.

Mangoes rotted.

Another year of brown blossoms.
No books opened at the pool.
My labor is a blank page

and my freedom is writer's block.

I am beginning to fear for my days.

Horses

I'm visiting the horses, he tells me on the phone.
It's Christmas and I am, as always,
visiting my parents. He is, as always, alone,
on Christmas, my husband
who is patient and kind and forgiving.

He did not grow up with horses, and I grew up afraid
of their memory. When the horse bit me
I was not afraid of it, but my mother was
and held me so tight it hurt and said
I could never see the horses again.

Years later, I am married to a patient and kind
and forgiving man who took me to visit the horses
and held my hand gently when I was afraid.
Now he visits the horses when he is alone.

He is alone at Christmas while I visit my parents
who insist that I talk about the horses
as if they own the horses and I am borrowing them.
You never liked horses, my mother says, tightly.

My husband brings carrots this time, and the horses
nip his pockets and lick the salt from his fingers.
I teach him to breathe into their nostrils.
He knows their sounds and listens to their moods.

They have learned to trust him through kindness and patience
and forgiveness, and he to trust them too. There is one
lost and tormented horse and she will nuzzle me
when I stroke her; gently, frightened.

I do not tell my parents that he visits the horses alone.
They know he is alone at Christmas.
I go home at Christmas to have them tell me what
I can never do, what I could never do.

Together, we visit the horses, my husband and I.
When I am afraid, he is patient and kind and forgiving.
Eventually, I stop
telling my parents about the horses.
This year I will stay with my husband at Christmas.

The Poetry

under my skin like crude, the bobbing of my pen
could render it, clean it up enough for consumption
to slowly kill its maker.

I do not want to be confessional.

The barge that clears the litter could be my verse.
My words an uncut plastic six-pack around my mother's neck.
I do not want to be confessional.

The poetry in me fights like the angry,
silent death of this galaxy.
It flares like the sun and my
communications are scrambled.
The storms get worse every year
that I don't try to teach others
what can happen
when the only thing
you want is an explanation.
Fear rips through a person like a tornado
and you fail to see the way it should be seen:

not as a confession but as a small, simple story.

That's what I want my poetry to be:

A small, simple story about a violent, beautiful world.

To Create

The deer bone that washed ashore, found
on the day I went North to kill myself, when
a man helped me
finally understand how history is a reason
to live.

Now these old bones, beside my body
so vivid with life, in the newest
place where I find solitude, given to me
as always, by a man who
doesn't question me or my place.

Trees, bones, churning space, these men
offer their spirit for me to take, offer without knowing,
never questioning, never doubting.

I come back to them again and
again: men and their talismans.
Men and trust and some small, grand piece of Earth:
waiting for the day I see the words they want me to write.

Marriage

You make me feel soft in good ways.

The Assisted Living Home, After Cancer Surgery

I am the hinge that keeps this family together.
They are neither the door nor the wall nor the air
moving between spaces. They are
what happens when the door is locked.

I am too scared, at first, to run, to cry, to whistle.
I creak like a rusty door in the darkness giving away
the intruder.
Across the hall from my mother is a dying man
with blind eyes and gurgling lungs and no family.
When it began to rot, they took out the thing that made me,
took my first home in my mother, where I claim to have felt
a watermelon seed drop on my head.

We arrived alongside a mental case, dead
as an empty sail, and I think of
Anne and her cigarettes and try
to remember my mother breastfeeding.

The door closes, and she shakes and he shakes and
it is too heavy to keep open, the hinge is too loose
and there is not enough air moving, breathing.
Everyone closes the door when they leave, leaving
us to our little prison. We lock our jaws and dream
of freedom, each with a separate dream of beauty,
each with our own reasons.

Journey/Wreckage

The sun came back around.
The Endurance was found.
Metaphors abound.

So This is Another Day

Going to your best friend's funeral
is like coming home from
war missing an arm.
You have a nightmare and
reach for the lamp with the ghost limb.

Going to your best friend's funeral
is a political subject.
It is abortion, gay marriage,
religion, race, and people look
past you when they touch your other arm,
the good one, the one that is still there.
You imagine slapping them with the missing
one, laugh at your own joke and look around
expecting a roadside bomb and your best friend's face.

Everyone is so calm and colorful
and fragile as the sand and gun smoke
that a grenade could blow away.
You are dressed as a civilian then,
and they don't even know about the
tanks and humvees, helicopters,
strange language, movies, CDs,
"I've drank out of you before,"
nicknames, jokes, confidences,
tears, laughs, stories
and the fact that you went to your best friend's funeral
today.

San Juan after the Hurricanes

I was not born here, but I was asked to live here
asked to help those who were born here
after they lost everything, including hope.

Hope is the hardest thing to get back.
Hope has a relationship with home.

Who are you when you don't have a home?

This was a paradise where I made myself

eat papaya for breakfast
every morning wearing nothing but a sarong.

All I wanted was oatmeal and sweatpants.

                        the coquí
Called to me like   the familiar

Every night, their song resetting my pulse

quickened by the fireworks
the cats in heat
the wind off the water whipping through
                passing over my bare skin
with the reminder of a spirit they call
                                Juracán.

The candles in the grocery store
mean a kind of magic I do not know.

I collect bougainvillea flowers.
Their petals are tissue-like and
I am homesick for the velvet of my roses.

Once, the waves were too much,
too constant and eternal
and I had to close the windows.
In the silence I could exist, I
could be anywhere in the world.
Home has a relationship with hope.

Boundaries

Social Media
makes me
feel
like a cyborg
with multiple personalities.

Waiting for the Cicadas to Sing

Dissociating through pleasure,
your memory in my fingers,
my skin warm, time as a being

when I cum I hear the first notes

stilted, off-rhythm, like a stretch
like eye-contact, like a lingering hug

so many books on the shelf,
so many untold stories.

We buried ours underground.

I have walked above these sleeping giants
for seventeen years, never knowing their dreams.

Underground, they dreamed of pleasure.

We buried our story underground,
a dream we will forget,
unless it awakens.

Pnyx

Speak the truth.
Truth has directions.

Write the law.
Law has matter.

Gather the crowd.
The crowd has magic.

There are gods, and there is power.

Advocate

Today I do not have the energy
to care for my roses.
The basil slumps in her pot.
Fear has a way of transmitting —
not through the eye, but
through the bones of the back
bent towards the maybe of hope.

Today I do not have the energy
to care for my roses because
I have already cared for the people
who have only my face, and their faith.

Today I do not have the energy
to care for my roses because I have
abandoned myself to care for
the people who only have faith.

They don't know about my roses
and they don't need to. No one
knows about them. When no one
has the energy to care
for me
my roses are what keep me safe.

Grief

The saffron crocuses bloomed
under the volunteer tomatoes.

*

That is the first line of a poem
I will write about you.

Another Surgery

Here the punishment fits
the crime: two feet of scars outside
her and miles inside me.

I have tried the expected dreams,
but now realize that the only one
to ever give me peace is the dream to flee.

Throw another peel on the flame.
I write for two things; love and misery.

I can see and hear
and smell and touch and taste
the corkscrew way that strangers
who will listen to a lie
are my only saving grace.

I chose to save my mother's life.
Chose words and loneliness,
to be unpublished and no one's wife.

Science

The opposite of death is not life;
The opposite of death is fertility.

Femininity

Pride was the grey on the fingertip
of my white glove
and the dirt on my shoe.

Pride was the bruise
my mother left on my arm
and the sleeve that hid it from view.

Pride was the wine
that got me the arms
and the money
that got me the roof.

Abandoned

The green shovel strikes a beam reach
from the castle ruins.
Nearby, sand spilling
from an overturned pail mirrors a morning puddle.
The smallest boy tipped a tricycle
and walked away, to kick a ball.
Another pair raced down the long stretch of black top,
where the blond girl won by a foot.
She screeched in triumph.

Inside the old canoe, a dark-skinned girl sat quietly
and pressed the keys of a yellow and red and green
plastic piano. Before that, she walked along the fence
dragging a stick against the rungs.
A group of girls baked a pile of leaves
in the toy oven. It involved many discussions.

The boy with the curls looped to the back of the line
after every turn on the swings.
Another took a Wiffle ball on the nose
and cried until he got a hug.
A beach ball sailed into the sandbox
then back to the jungle gym.

The tiny blue wheelbarrow, still full of mulch,
came to rest beside the slide
when the grown-ups called them back inside again.

An hour ago
I watched all this happen
from my window above the playground.

Regret

It is possible
> that you loved me.

It is possible
> that thinking about me
> comforted you.

It is possible
> that in the peace of imagination
> you dreamed of parallel navigation.

It is possible
> that now
> in company or solitude
> you are also remembering
> how we are both, unforgiven.

About the Author

Carrie Carter is a poet living and working in Washington, DC. She holds a BA in English from The Ohio State University. *High Water* (Quillkeepers Press, 2023) is her debut publication and includes work written over twenty years. Also in 2023, Carrie is a contributor and sponsor in a gun violence protest anthology produced by Gnashing Teeth Press. Carrie is a non-traditional professional, working in various industries, including retail, academia, facilities, and community advocacy. When she is not reading or writing poetry, she can be found in her garden, telling the bees that she loves them.

About the Cover Designer

David Wojciechowski is a freelance graphic designer living in Albany, NY. He has designed books and journals for Deep Vellum, Ricochet Editions, *Salt Hill*, Split/Lip Press, and others. David is also the author of the poetry collection *Dreams I Never Told You & Letters I Never Sent* (Gold Wake Press, 2017) and the chapbook *Koniec (End)* (Greying Ghost, 2023). His second full-length collection is coming in 2024 from ELJ Editions.

He can be found online at davidwojo.com or on Twitter and Instagram @MrWojoRising.

Other Titles by Quillkeepers Press

Dislocated — A full length collection of Poetry by Dylan Webster

The Matador's Wife — A chapbook length collection of poetry by Andrés Colón

Scars & lyres — A chapbook length collection of poetry by ww harris

My West — A chapbook length collection of poetry by Jenifer Fox

Notable Moons — A Chapbook length collection of poetry by David Gunton

Botany of Gaia — A nature inspired anthology of poetry, memoirs, essays, and short stories by various artist

Turning Dark into Light: and Other Magic Tricks of the Mind — A mental health anthology of poetry, memoirs, essays, and short stories by various artist

Bare Bones — A Halloween themed anthology of poetry, memoirs, essays, and short stories by various artist

Inspired — *An art inpired by art fan-fic anthology of* poetry, memoirs, essays, and short stories by various artist

Rearing in the Rearview — *A parenting themed* anthology of poetry, memoirs, essays, and short stories by various artist

www.ingramcontent.com/pod-product-compliance
Lightning Source LLC
Chambersburg PA
CBHW070453130626
46553CB00006B/2396